Secrets
of
Serenity

A Treasury of Inspiration

D0342182

A Running Press Miniature Edition™
Copyright © 1996 by Running Press.

Printed in China.

Library of Congress Cataloging-in-Publication Number
95–69317

ISBN 978-1-56138-690-1

This book may be ordered by mail from the publisher.
Please include $1.00 for postage and handling.
But try your bookstore first!

Running Press Book Publishers
2300 Chestnut Street
Philadelphia, PA 19103-4371

Visit us on the web!
www.runningpress.com

Contents

The more complicated and uncertain life is, the more we yearn for tranquility, with time enough to love, play, work, and think. We want to enjoy the simple things—conversation, snowfall, laughter. Overwhelmed by the intensity of our lives, we want to simply *be*, but often we don't know how to begin.

We are not alone in our search for serenity. Inside this little book are the inspiring thoughts of writers, philosophers, scholars, theologians, and leaders who have sought—and found—the secrets of serenity. Let their words of wisdom guide you as you search for peace and tranquility in your own heart, mind, and soul.

Serenity
of the
Heart

How simple and frugal a thing is happiness: a glass of wine, a roast chestnut, a wretched little brazier, the sound of the sea. . . . All that is required to feel that here and now is happiness is a simple, frugal heart.

—Nikos Kazantzakis
(1885–1957)
Greek writer

To be content with what we possess
is the greatest and most secure
of riches.

—Marcus Tullius Cicero
(106–43 B.C.)
Roman orator,
statesman,
and philosopher

We know the truth, not only by the reason, but by the heart.

—Blaise Pascal
(1623–1662)
French mathematician
and philosopher

It is only with the heart
that one can see rightly;
what is essential is
invisible to the eye.

—Antoine de Saint-Exupéry
(1900–1944)
French aviator
and writer

Be not satisfied with partial contentment, for he who engulfs the spring
of life with one empty jar will
depart with two full jars.

—Kahlil Gibran
(1883–1931)
Lebanese poet, novelist,
essayist, and artist

Serenity of the Heart

The heart of the wise man lies quiet
like limpid water.

—Cameroonian saying

Don't hurry, don't worry. You're only here for a short visit. So be sure to stop and smell the flowers.

—Walter C. Hagen
(1892–1969)
American golfer

When the book of life is opening,
our readings are secret.

—E. M. Forster
(1879–1970)
English writer

Better are loaves when the heart is
joyous, than riches in unhappiness.

—Amenemope
(c. 12th-century B.C.)
Egyptian writer

The highest form of bliss is living
with a certain degree of folly.

—Desiderius Erasmus
(c. 1466–1536)
Dutch scholar

Life is not always what one wants
it to be, but to make the best of it as
it is, is the only way of being happy.

—Jennie Churchill
(1854–1921)
English editor and
playwright

Happiness is not a state to arrive at,
but a manner of traveling.

—Margaret Lee Runbeck
20th-century
American writer

Many search for happiness as we
look for a hat we wear on our heads.

—Nikolaus Lenau
  [Nikolaus Franz]
  (1802–1850)
  Austrian poet

To be without some of the things
you want is an indispensable part
of happiness.

—Bertrand Russell
(1872–1970)
English mathematician
and philosopher

He is richest who is content with the least; for content is the wealth of nature.

—Socrates
(c. 470–399 B.C.)
Greek philosopher

To be content with little is hard,
to be content with much impossible.

—Baronness Marie von
Ebner-Eschenbach
(1830–1916)
Austrian writer
and poet

The more passions and desires
one has, the more ways one has
of being happy.

—Charlotte-Catherine
17th-century
Princess of Monaco

If you want others to be happy,
practice compassion. If you want to
be happy, practice compassion.

—Dalai Lama
(b. 1935)
Tibetan religious leader
American essayist and poet

Happiness is reflective, like the
light of heaven.

—Washington Irving
(1783–1859)
American writer
and poet

Accentuate the positive,
eliminate the negative....

—Johnny Mercer
(1909–1976)
American
songwriter

One must marry one's feelings to
one's beliefs and ideas. That is
probably the only way to achieve
a measure of harmony in
one's life.

—Etty Hillesum
(1914–1943)
Dutch diarist

If a man does not keep pace with his companions, perhaps it is because he hears a different drummer. Let him step to the music which he hears, however measured or far away.

—Henry David Thoreau
(1817–1862)
American writer

As he thinketh in his heart, so is he.

—*Proverbs 23:7*

There is a wisdom of the head,
and . . . a wisdom of the heart.

—Charles Dickens
(1812–1870)
English writer

Make the most of every sense; glory
in all of the pleasures and beauty
which the world reveals to you. . . .

—Helen Keller
(1880–1968)
American writer and
lecturer

If you want to be happy, be.

—Aleksey
Konstantinovich
Tolstoy
(1817–1875)
Russian writer

Serenity
of the
Mind

Seek out the good and your mind
will fill with happiness.

—John Marks Templeton
20th-century American
financier

. . . happiness doesn't depend upon
who you are or what you have;
it depends solely upon what
you think.

—Dale Carnegie
(1888–1955)
American writer
and speaker

The real things haven't changed.
It is still best to be honest and truth-
ful; to make the most of what we
have; to be happy with simple
pleasures; and have courage when
things go wrong.

—Laura Ingalls Wilder
(1867–1957)
American writer

If you can't change your fate,
change your attitude.

—Amy Tan
(b. 1952)
American writer

People create their own questions because they're afraid to look straight. All you have to do is look straight and see the road, and when you see it, don't sit looking at it—walk.

—Ayn Rand
(1905–1982)
Russian-born American
writer

There is no other door to knowledge
than the door Nature opens; and
there is no truth except the truths
we discover in Nature.

—Luther Burbank
(1849–1926)
American horticulturist

Life is not a problem to be solved
but a reality to be experienced.

—Søren Kierkegaard
(1813–1855)
Danish philosopher

Life just is. You have to flow with it.
Give yourself to the moment.
Let it happen.

> —Jerry Brown
> (b. 1938)
> American politician

I have a simple philosophy. Fill what's empty. Empty what's full. Scratch where it itches.

—Alice Roosevelt
Longworth
(1884–1980)
American hostess

Be content with such things
as ye have.

—Hebrews 13:5

Happiness is when what you think, what you say, and what you do are in harmony.

—Mohandas Gandhi
(1869–1948)
Indian statesman

It is the mind that maketh good of
ill, that maketh wretch or happy,
rich or poor.

—Edmund Spenser
(c. 1552–1599)
English poet

Life is a mirror and will reflect
back to the thinker what he thinks
into it.

—Ernest Holmes
(1887–1960)
American writer
and philosopher

When one's thoughts are neither
frivolous nor flippant, when one's
thoughts are neither stiff-necked nor
stupid, but rather, are harmonious—
they habitually render physical calm
and deep insight.

—Hildegard von Bingen
(1098–1179)
German religious leader

Like water which can clearly mirror
the sky and the trees only so long as
its surface is undisturbed, the mind
can only reflect the true image
of the Self when it is tranquil and
wholly relaxed.

—Indra Devi
    20th-century
    Russian-born
    American writer

I am I plus my circumstances.

—José Ortega y Gasset
(1883–1955)
Spanish philosopher
and writer

A happy person is not a person
in a certain set of circumstances,
but rather a person with a certain
set of attitudes.

—Hugh Downs
(b. 1921)
American journalist

Circumstances and situations do color life but you have been given the mind to choose what the color shall be.

—John Homer Miller
(b. 1904)
American writer
and educator

All fortune belongs to him who
has a contented mind. Is not the
whole earth covered with leather
for him whose feet are encased
in shoes?

—from the
Panchatantra
2nd-century B.C.
collection of Hindu
tales

The secret of contentment is knowing how to enjoy what you have, and to be able to lose all desire for things beyond your reach.

—Lin Yutang
(1895–1976)
Chinese writer

The mind is its own place, and
in itself can make a heaven of
Hell, a hell of Heaven.

—John Milton
(1608–1674)
English poet

Serenity of the Mind

It matters not how strait the gate,

How charged with punishments
   the scroll,

I am the master of my fate:

I am the captain of my soul.

> —William Henley
> (1849–1903)
> English editor,
> playwright, and poet

. . . we are the masters of our fate, the captains of our souls, *because* we have the power to control our thoughts.

—Napoleon Hill
(c. 1883–1970)
American writer

The mind is the master over every kind of fortune: itself acts in both ways, being the cause of its own happiness and misery.

—Seneca
(c. 4 B.C.–A.D. 65)
Roman statesman
and philosopher

When everything has its proper place in our minds, we are able to stand in equilibrium with the rest of the world.

—Henri Frédéric Amiel
(1821–1881)
Swiss philosopher
and poet

The goal of all civilization, all religious thought, and all that sort of thing is simply to have a Good Time. But man gets so solemn over the process that he forgets the end.

—Don Marquis
(1878–1937)
American writer

Life is not a matter of holding
good cards, but of playing a poor
hand well.

—Robert Louis Stevenson
(1850–1894)
Scottish writer and poet

What fates impose, that men must
needs abide;
It boots not to resist both wind
and tide.

—William Shakespeare
(1564–1616)
English playwright
and poet

To keep a lamp burning we have to keep putting oil in it.

—Mother Teresa of Calcutta
(1910–1997)
Founder, Missionaries
of Charity

Sometimes I sits and thinks, and
sometimes I just sits.

—Satchel Paige
(c. 1906–1982)
American baseball
player

Never be afraid to sit awhile
and think.

—Lorraine Hansberry
(1930–1965)
American playwright

We are what we think. All that we are arises with our thoughts. With our thoughts, we make the world.

—Siddhārtha Guatama
[The Buddha]
(c. 563–483 B.C.)
Prince of the Sākyas and
founder of Buddhism

Thoughts are energy. And you
can make your world or break
your world by your thinking.

—Susan L. Taylor
(b. 1946)
American journalist

It is the mind that rules the body.

—Sojourner Truth
   (c. 1797–1883)
   American evangelist
   and reformer

Whoever knocks persistently,
ends by entering.

—Ali (600–661)
Arabian caliph

The universe is change; our life is
what our thoughts make it.

—Marcus Aurelius
Antoninus
(121–180)
Roman emperor

I accept the universe!

—Margaret Fuller
(1810–1850)
American critic and
social reformer

It's good to be just plain happy;
it's a little better to know that you're
happy; but to understand that you're
happy and to know why and how . . .
and still be happy, be happy in the
being and the knowing, well that is
beyond happiness, that is bliss.

—Henry Miller
(1891–1980)
American writer

Serenity
of the
Soul

Seek not to understand that you may believe, but believe that you may understand.

—Saint Augustine
(354–430)
Christian philosopher

Some people think that as soon as
you plant a tree, it must bear fruit.
We must allow it to grow a bit.

—Prince Tunku Putra
　　Abdul Rahman
　　(b. 1903)
　　Malaysian political leader

Learn to be quiet enough to hear
the sound of the genuine within
yourself so that you can hear it
in others.

—Marian Wright Edelman
(b. 1939)
American writer

We need time to dream, time to remember, and time to reach the infinite. Time to be.

—Gladys Taber
(1899–1980)
American writer

Whenever you are sincerely pleased,
you are nourished.

—Ralph Waldo Emerson
(1803–1882)
American essayist
and poet

Where there is peace and
meditation, there is neither
anxiety nor doubt.

—Saint Francis of Assisi
(c. 1181–1226)
Italian friar

Peace, she supposed, was contingent
upon a certain disposition of the
soul, a disposition to receive the gift
that only detachment from self
made possible.

—Elizabeth Goudge
(1900–1984)
English writer
and artist

The transcendental state of Being
lies beyond all seeing, hearing,
touching, smelling, and tasting—
beyond all thinking and beyond
all feeling.

—Maharishi Mahesh Yogi
20th-century Indian
transcendentalist
and educator

Manifest plainness,
Embrace simplicity,
Reduce selfishness,
Have few desires.

—Lao Tzu
(c. 604–531 B.C.)
Chinese founder
of Taoism

It is the chiefest point of happiness that a man is willing to be what he is.

—Desiderius Erasmus
(c. 1466–1536)
Dutch scholar

The strong, calm man is always
loved and revered. He is like a
shade-giving tree in a thirsty land,
or a sheltering rock in a storm.

—James Allen
(1864–1912)
English writer

God has made many doors opening
into truth which He opens to all
who knock upon them with hands
of faith.

—Kahlil Gibran
(1883–1931)
Lebanese poet, novelist,
essayist, and artist

'Twant me, 'twas the Lord. I always told him, "I trust to you. I don't know where to go or what to do, but I expect you to lead me," and he always did.

—Harriet Tubman
(c. 1820–1913)
American abolitionist

God, give us grace to accept with serenity the things that cannot be changed, courage to change the things which should be changed, and the wisdom to distinguish the one from the other.

—Reinhold Niebuhr
(1892–1971)
American cleric
and theologian

Your life is like a tapestry, being
woven by God and history on an
enchanted loom. Every bobble
of the shuttle has meaning, every
thread is important.

—Richard Nelson Bolles
(b. 1927)
American writer
and educator

Give me beauty in the inward soul;
may the outward and the inward
man be at one.

—Socrates
   (c. 470–399 B.C.)
   Greek philosopher

Peace is the fairest form
of happiness.

—William Ellery Channing
(1780–1842)
American cleric

The goal of life is living in
agreement with nature.

—Zeno of Citium
(335–263 B.C.)
Greek philosopher

. . . this was the simple happiness
of complete harmony with her
surroundings, the happiness that
asks for nothing, that just accepts,
just breathes, just is.

—Countess Van Arnim
(1866–1941)
English writer

We must walk in balance on the earth—a foot in spirit and a foot in the physical.

—Lynn Andrews
20th-century American
writer and shaman

To become a happy person, have a clean soul, eyes that see romance in the commonplace, a child's heart, and spiritual simplicity.

—Norman Vincent Peale
(1898–1993)
American cleric
and writer

Every man's life is a fairy-tale written by God's fingers.

—Hans Christian Andersen
(1805–1875)
Danish writer

It is when you are really living in the present—working, thinking, lost, absorbed in something you care about very much, that you are living spiritually.

—Brenda Ueland
(1891–1985)
American writer, editor,
and educator

Our physical body and the see-and-touch world are not life, but only one step on our spirit's journey.

—Paul Pearsall
  20th-century American educator

To everything there is a season,
and a time to every purpose
under heaven.

—*Ecclesiastes 3:1*

The past is but the beginning of a beginning, and all that is and has been is but the twilight of the dawn.

—H. G. Wells
(1866–1946)
English writer,
sociologist,
and historian

Let nothing disturb thee,
Nothing affright thee;
All things are passing;
God never changeth.

—Saint Teresa of Avila
(1515–1582)
Spanish poet and nun

No pain, no palm; no thorns, no throne; no gall, no glory; no cross, no crown.

—William Penn
(1633–1718)
English religious
reformer and colonialist

Although the world is very full of suffering, it is also full of the over-coming of it.

—Helen Keller
(1880–1968)
American writer and
lecturer

Secrets of Serenity

We must live through the dreary winter
If we would value the spring;
And the woods must be cold and silent
Before the robins sing.
The flowers must be buried in darkness
Before they can bud and bloom,
And the sweetest, warmest sunshine
Comes after the storm and gloom.

—Anonymous

In the depths of winter, I finally
learned that within me there lay an
invincible summer.

—Albert Camus
(1913–1960)
French writer
and philosopher

Nothing can bring you peace but yourself. Nothing can bring you peace but the triumph of principles.

—Ralph Waldo Emerson
(1803–1882)
American essayist
and poet

Peace is the evening star of the soul,
as virtue is its sun, and the two are
never far apart.

—Charles Caleb Colton
(1780–1832)
English cleric

We shall find peace.
We shall hear the angels,
we shall see the sky
sparkling with diamonds.

—Anton Chekhov
(1860–1904)
Russian writer

Photography Credits

This book has been bound using
handcraft methods, and Smyth-sewn
to ensure durability.

The dust jacket and interior were
designed by Ken Newbaker.

Photo research by Susan Oyama.

Cover photograph by Chuck Kuhn.

The text was set in Adobe Garamond and
Bureau Garamond Light.